A Child's War

A Child's War

*The German Occupation
of Guernsey as seen
through young eyes ...*

Molly Bihet

AMBERLEY

First published in 1985 by Molly Bihet

This edition published 2009

Amberley Publishing
Cirencester Road, Chalford,
Stroud, Gloucestershire, GL6 8PE

www.amberley-books.com

British Library Cataloguing in Publication Data.
A catalogue record for this book is available from the British Library.

ISBN 978 1 84868 205 4

Typesetting and origination by Amberley Publishing
Printed in Great Britain

This is dedicated to my dear mother, Gladys Finigan,
who was always caring and cheerful to everyone
and an inspiration to all who knew her
in those dark days of 1940 to 1945.

Preface

This is a simple story in my own words of happenings to myself and my family, as I remember them, during the Occupation of Guernsey from 1940 to 1945. Being nearly 9 years old in June 1940, my memories are vivid, mainly during the last three years when I was a pupil of the State's Intermediate School. These years, apart from the evacuation, were the most eventful, although I do remember very clearly all the events I have written about. I wanted to express my feelings during these difficult years of German rule and the different games and unusual pastimes of a child done solely because we were hungry and restricted. Our school days and friends were very special at this time. The 'happenings' of our nine in family and friends were unusual, sometimes frightening and now can seem funny. This book, hopefully, will give you an insight of how I felt during 'a child's war' and how I felt at being free on Liberation Day when I was nearly 14 years old.

When I tell you I received a kick from 'Otto', a Nazi, and after the Liberation I received a letter from Mr. Winston Churchill, this surely will make a 'different' story. I was so proud then and proud now, having been born (gratefully too!) in our beautiful Island of Guernsey along with all my family before me.

Before closing, I must thank my husband and two daughters who have encouraged me to write my story, but who I'm sure are also relieved and thankful that after talking of completing it for so long it is now finished!

Contents

Foreword

It gives me great pleasure to write this Foreword to *A Child's War* by Molly Bihet.

I have known Molly all her life and her mother all my life. I have then read this book with the greatest interest. In writing the book Molly has rendered a great service to our Island and to posterity by placing on record the fateful years of the German Occupation as seen through the extremely perspective and extremely penetrating eyes of a very young and typical Guernsey school girl.

The Occupation years were long, bitter and agonising. We all lived on a knife edge not knowing from day to day what next would happen and always in danger and appalling difficulties in the long struggle for the very survival of the life of our community.

The Occupation did result in one great and inestimable blessing. In adversity may be but it drew our people more closely together than ever before and knitted them into one large and united family. It was a family which resisted to the fullest extent possible that Occupation and a family burning as ever with the fiercest pride of patriotism and of their Island and its heritage which the Occupation could never hope to weaken.

All this Molly brings out so clearly and so movingly in her book which should have a place of honour in the homes of all Guernsey men and Guernsey women.

Sir John Loveridge, Kt., C.B.E.
Bailiff of Guernsey 1973 to 1982
May 1985

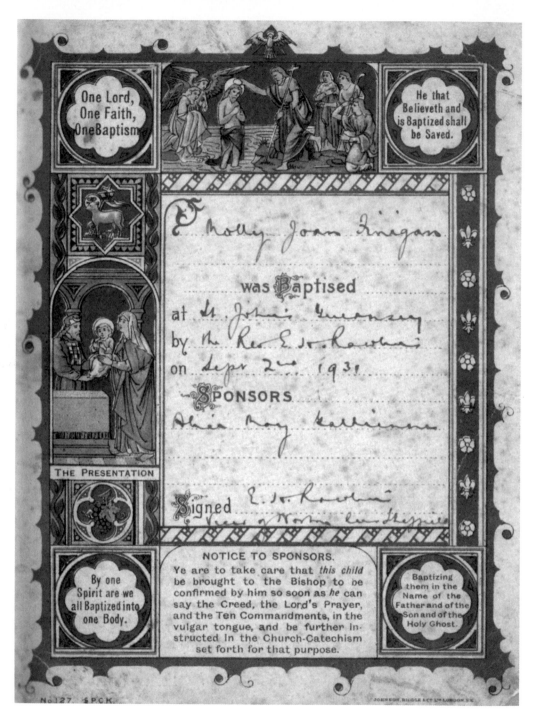

The author's birth certificate.

Acknowledgements

Many thanks to Carel Toms for permission to reproduce certain photographs and also to Mr. Richard Heaume of the Guernsey Occupation Museum, the Court Library and the Priaulx Library of St. Peter Port.

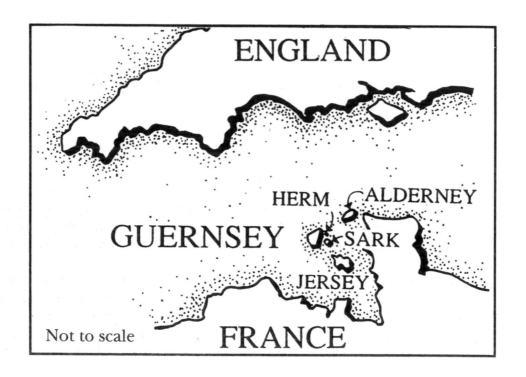

The location of Guernsey and the other Channel Islands, in relation to England and France.

Chapter One

EVACUATION. YES OR NO?

On this dark dreary morning I can recall so many memories of the German Occupation of Guernsey. My mother and I often sat and laughed about past experiences; but it was no laughing matter at the time to my dear mother and father and all parents who had children to worry and care about for five long years.

My memories began when I was eight, my sister was six and we were a very ordinary happy family living in a pleasant house overlooking the beautiful harbour of St. Peter Port. I remember the talk of the 'war' but it did not mean much to girls of my age. I was just old enough to knit socks and helmets at school and to bring my knitting home, all for the men going to the front.

I knew my mother and father were worried about the war and there was much talk among the grown-ups. Dad was of 'call up' age and we wondered whether he would have to leave us to go and fight.

It was not long after this I remember my mother and father were more concerned as all the children were expected to leave the island as the German Enemy Forces had moved on into France.

I remember all the talk to friends and relations "are you going?" or "are you going to stay?", "what are we going to do?"—the phone kept ringing and Mum and Dad were very worried as to what was going to happen to us all.

If parents wanted their children to go to England with the school, special arrangements had been made and they had to 'report' at their school at a given time and be prepared ready to join the ships and leave.

At Burnt Lane and St. Joseph's Schools (the Junior and Senior Catholic Schools) all had to assemble at St. Joseph's School—my husband, André,

Best Wishes XMAS 1939

Molly's school photograph, at Burnt Lane School, St. Peter Port.

who was twelve at the time remembers going with his mother very early (around 4–5am) in the morning to the school, saying goodbye there, then walking down with teachers to the harbour.

He remembers being lined up like all the other children in particular school groups, being checked, then getting on board. Other parents were given the time to report with their children down at the harbour and leave the children in the care of school teachers. Then parents had to decide whether they would follow on to the mainland. All grown-ups were being advised to leave as soon as possible and there were to be thousands of Islanders evacuated.

It was the talk of everyone but what a difficult decision to make. Leaving their homes probably for the first time ever—in those days in the 1930's it was an occasion to cross the water and spend a day on 'Herm'—a thirty minute boat trip! Now the Islanders were being advised to leave their homes and cross the water for an indefinite period!

The reason why my parents hesitated in leaving and there was so much tension and worry was because there were six in the family at our home 'Rose Villa' at Les Canichers.

Firstly my old Grandfather (Pop Collins as he was known and quite a character as you will hear later) was over seventy and had been born at Rose Villa and being very stubborn was definitely not going to leave his home for anyone! Least of all for Germans!

In fact, my sister and I, also my mother and her two sisters and three brothers had also been born at 'Rose Villa', the house we lived in. My uncle, Reg Collins (my mother's brother) whom my mother also looked after had been wounded in the First World War and still had a bullet lodged in his spine. He had a stiff leg and had difficulty walking well—so he also had made up his mind, he was staying! This left my father to decide, he was running a small building business—he felt he ought to stay a little longer to sort things out and to look after 'Pop' and Reg. He desperately wanted my mother to leave with my sister and I, and catch the boat for the mainland and he would follow as soon as he could.

The threat of the invasion seemed to loom nearer but still so much uncertainty, no-one knew what to do for the best. I can well remember leaving home around 6am with gas masks around our necks, some small carrier bags with small items of clothing and some cash carefully hidden— sewn inside our vests. 'Just in case', said Mum, but three times we returned as my mother was not allowed to travel with the school teachers and children. If Mum had permitted us to leave without her, she must have felt in her heart that Joyce and I would have had to separate as we were attending different schools at the time. She must have kept hoping that the next time could see us being allowed to travel together. Yet again we tried, each time I was crying wanting to stay with my father, my sister was crying wanting to go on the big boat and my mother I'm sure was very concerned and confused. No wonder my mother did not want to be parted from us, we were only 6 and 8 years old and being a mother now I can well understand a little how she felt. Nevertheless after the fourth attempt the decision was made for us!—we just had to stay and the evacuation came to a complete stop.

THEY'VE LANDED!

On the lovely afternoon of 28th June, 1940 we were in the road looking out over the harbour when planes came very low over the sea and harbour— we gave them a wave with a cucumber we'd just bought from a shop nearby but soon ran for shelter as they were German planes which started to machine-gun and bomb the ships and the harbour. We ran for shelter down some steps opposite our house and into a long corridor in the basement of a friend's house called 'Grangeclare'. There were several of us there and we were all very frightened. The harbour was so close to where we were sheltering and we had never heard anything like it before. It seemed ages before the noise of the explosions and machine gunning stopped. Eventually we came up to the road where we had originally been standing waving and we could see that there must be terrible damage as everywhere seemed to be ablaze and smoking.

Clearly we could see the extent of the air raid. There were carts and lorries burnt out, which had been loaded with tomatoes ready to he shipped to the mainland, and boats bombarded. Our beautiful harbour had been transformed. Mum and Dad were very worried that Uncle Reg could be hurt or maybe killed—he could not run and, with a stiff leg, had much difficulty moving quickly and he was working down the harbour at the time. He eventually came home not hurt but very shocked and saddened. Thankfully, he managed to get under the jetty in time. Later we knew fully of the deaths and injuries the Germans had caused. 34 civilians had been killed and many injured.

Very soon (30th June) we realised the enemy had landed, with no fuss, very quietly, but we were all a little frightened. My mother decided to stay indoors—she did not want to face the enemy and wondered whether they were square-headed as we had heard! It was over a month later when she decided to leave the house and although still nervous decided the Germans did really look like normal human beings after all!

There was one main worry, had all the children left? My mother and father just kept wondering if my sister and I were the only children left on the island, so many full boatloads of people (mostly children) had gone, could there be any families left like us? Well, thankfully there was and after

The Weighbridge Clock Tower after being hit by a bomb.

the dismay and the tension of the past few days—there were many friends still on the island. What a great relief for my parents knowing this. Come what may, we were all in the same boat so to speak.

My father's two brothers, Ted and Jack, and Ted's teenage son had also stayed on alone sending their wives and other children away but it wasn't very long before they realised they just couldn't manage on their own and they asked whether they could live with us. My mother, being the very kind person she was, could not refuse and in a short while our family had grown from six to nine and out of this number four of the six men were over 6 feet tall and very big eaters! In the early part of the Occupation, stocks were fairly plentiful and my mother tried to buy in as much as she could—not to be greedy but thought if the war and Occupation lasted for 6 months, at least we'd have 'a little something' in the cupboard. The few tins and packets we had of tea, sugar etc. soon dwindled but Mum tried to keep a tin of meat or fruit for a special occasion. Of course, if the Occupation had only lasted for six months we would have fared quite well, but as it was a very long six months the 'little something' we had did not last and the many special occasions outweighed our few tins and packets, especially having six hungry males and two growing daughters to bring up, and looking back now I wonder now how she managed it! I suppose black marketing helped as it wasn't long before our weekly food ration was small and gradually getting smaller. Mum and Dad had to spend savings at these small barter shops that sprung up in the town either exchanging items or buying items of food if one was lucky at the very beginning for a £1, but with goods getting more scarce as time went by, these items, such as a ¼ of tea, would cost £7 or £8. £1 was a lot of money in those days but Mum had her money's worth! The precious packet of tea was dried and brewed several times as you can imagine, and nothing was wasted. Everything was precious when it came to food. FOOD! That's the main topic I seem to remember.

Burnt out lorries loaded with tomatoes which should have been sent to the mainland. Many of the workmen and drivers were killed sheltering underneath the lorries. 54 vehicles were burnt out completely, with 34 killed and 69 injured. There was much damage at the Weighbridge and all along the front and esplanade.

Soon after being occupied, barbed wire kept Islanders away from most of St Peter Port Harbour. The slipway is the Connaught Landing on the Albert Pier.

This photograph was taken from Les Cotils (Blue Mountains) from the gun emplacements just above our home. Castle Cornet is shown between the camouflaged netting and the back of the Royal Hotel is shown centrally on the sea-front, near the Weighbridge.

The Royal Hotel was the main military office of the German Commandant and those in charge.

Chapter Two

SCHOOL DAYS

School was the other all important part of the Occupation for me, but I must say that during these five years my school days were very happy. At the start of the war, and of the Occupation, I was attending Burnt Lane Catholic School, after a short time when the schools reopened, the pupils from Burnt Lane were transferred to Vauvert School, an Elementary School. My recollections here were happy, I can remember mixing very well with girls and boys alike, and Joyce and I were now together to attend the same school for over two years. Some of the children we knew from Burnt Lane School (Notre Dame du Rosaire) and some who were originally at the Vauvert School, after being organised we just formed one school. The evacuation of schoolchildren and their teachers must have caused many headaches for the Education Committee as several schools had to merge together.

I remember very little at this time except for the teachers and many nice friends we made and often see on the Island now.

During my days at Vauvert School the German Authorities allowed the schoolchildren a glass of milk during our morning break. I always wanted to be chosen to help allocate this for if there was any milk over after everyone had had their ration the helpers could have an extra glass!

At Vauvert School the top floor was out of bounds to the scholars, as flour was stored there for the German troops also part of the ground floor housed many of the 'wireless' sets that had been called in from the local population. Later the school was taken over completely by the Germans for storage and children were transferred to another school for the duration.

When I was 11 years old I entered an examination and was lucky to pass to the 'Occupation Intermediate School'. This was like going 'back home' to me as the Intermediate was then at the old Burnt Lane School. This again was to be a mixed school with many of the children being former pupils of the Intermediate Schools and Colleges of the Island. The children's ages ranged from 10 to 14 or 15 years and it was being run along the same lines as a grammar school. The schoolchildren here also were allowed a glass of milk during the morning break and whilst at the Intermediate we were also given a biscuit! I don't think we had seen a biscuit for at least two years when out of the blue we were handed one with our milk! These biscuits apparently were a gift from the French. I cannot remember how long we enjoyed this treat or how often but remember very well Mr. Mauger, our caretaker, having pleasure, and with a glint in his eyes, handing us our daily ration. I was also allowed cod liver oil every day at school during the latter part. Regular checks on our weight and health were made as many of us were underweight for our height.

Nearby our school was the Church of Notre Dame du Rosaire where the Sisters of the Church lived and they must have co-operated with the school as they provided us with a very nourishing soup three times a week.

The highlight of the day was queuing for our dish of bean soup which the kind nuns had prepared and cooked. We queued in an orderly fashion and when our turn came to be in the front all our attention was on the person in front, holding the bowl out, and just hoping the ladle was not lowered too much with either the girl or boy acquiring all the beans from the bottom! Families living in the town just could not buy vegetables easily so having a nice home-made vegetable soup three times a week was a luxury and something we all looked forward to. We had the headmaster, Mr. Peter Girard, to thank for getting us those precious beans and vegetables and they, in turn, came from several sources. All friends who wanted to help the children get some nourishment.

At the Intermediate School the German language had to be taught and naturally had to be a very important lesson. It was a compulsory lesson from the very start, by order!

I can well remember being questioned by a German Officer who used to visit the school quite regularly (but not too often, I'm glad to say!) to check on our progress. He used to stand in front of the class and just point at random and showed much pleasure when we answered correctly in the German language. There was always a prize every year for the scholar with high marks, also at one prize giving two German Officers were present and we were taught a special German song that had to be included during the ceremonies. Good second-hand books were given out as prizes and we were grateful and pleased if we received one. The school committee did their very best for us always.

There was one incident that must have caused Mr. Girard and the school committee some embarrassment and concern. At one stage two senior girls

Occupation States Intermediate School, 1943.

wanted to be excused from learning the language as they were preparing for their 'school certificate' and felt that time spent on learning German was wasted as they were not including this subject in their exam. This they were allowed to do, but then a little later on the other scholars in their class decided they too did not want to learn German either and they, being determined, felt very strongly about giving it up!

This refusal by the pupils must have caused some difficulties with the German authorities as I am sure Mrs. Tate, our German teacher, would have had to report any serious disruptions such as this. With discussions all round, this was all happily sorted out and the class resumed with the 'Deutsch'. The outcome must have pleased our teacher, Mrs. Tate, who was German herself and who indeed was a very fiery character and who definitely would not have liked being put out in any way!

Pupils came from all over the Island and seeing as there was no transport for them, they either had to walk or cycle to school. I only had a 15 minute walk up through the town to Burnt Lane School; so I was lucky. Everyone on the Island seemed to have a cycle, but where they came from was a mystery. A lot of them seemed to have been made with many spare parts and bits and pieces, others hadn't seen daylight for years I'm sure. We used to laugh at our friends' cycles for when the tyres needed to be replaced, hose pipes and ropes were bought to be used together to form a 'tyre'. This of course was a very bumpy ride for the scholars, some had to come from the Forest, or St. Saviours, but it was funny for us to watch them go off k-clump k-clump along the road! You can imagine this I'm sure.

The other clatter we heard constantly at school was the wooden-soled shoes we had to wear. I can remember having to wear these shoes, but once I was excited as I was offered a pair of boy's shoes with leather soles, and also a second hand warm navy blue coat! These items came from the Red Cross at Clifton through Miss Moon, one of our teachers. Most of the shoes were issued and given out from the Elizabeth College, many of us were excited in getting these 'different' wooden shoes, but in time most of us had to take foot exercises as the tendency was for us to have 'flat feet'.

One of the main interests at school during the Occupation were the leaflets that were brought into the school on the quiet! These leaflets with up-to-date news of the war were dropped into the country by British planes and brought in by the boys and girls and shown around the classroom. I often wondered if the teachers read and knew of these! I am sure they must have, but luckily our class were not caught red-handed at any time!

All of the reports were true information on how the war was progressing and we used to feel so important going home and giving the family all the latest news and also telling the tales of how the leaflets found their way to school. It was mainly the boys who used to bring them in as they would clamber into fields, over hedges and up trees if they spotted anything resembling paper. One such boy, Tom Jehan, who was in my class, did just that. One day he climbed up high into a tree to get the leaflet, struggled to get there and then clambered down to get on his bike but also found a German Officer was waiting for him below! There was nothing else for him to do but to get down and hand over his prize! We can laugh about it now but at the time it was frightening for Tom! He certainly had a glum face telling us all, but he never gave up searching.

Another time when I am sure there must have been a class full of glum faces was when Mr. Girard entered a classroom to find 'leaflets' hanging up to dry! No-one would own up that they had brought them in on this particular wet rainy day, but what a surprise for any teacher to find such 'washing on the line'! After a discussion with Rev. Frossard, who was teaching the class at the time, they were collected and taken away and nothing more was heard of the matter. Now one can understand the predicament and concern of any teacher, especially the headmaster finding these on the school premises, as anyone being found with one leaflet in their possession would have been very serious indeed. There must have been great worry and responsibilities on school teachers at this time because, as children, we could not really appreciate the consequences of any actions against the enemy (see page 32).

All this time the teachers were very understanding and if I remember rightly did not push us too hard. Strangely enough, it was only our German female teacher who had a very quick fiery temper and who used it! Many ex-pupils I am sure will remember her and the book hitting our heads and many other items being thrown at us! The headmaster and all the other teachers made up for her though and we had many kindnesses and much help from them. Looking back and thinking about those days, they were very special days and we were at a very special school. We were all confined in one area so to speak and, being a small number, we all knew each other. How many people can look back at a school photograph of 40 years ago and name all but one or two of the 110 pupils? I am sure many of the ex-pupils could, like myself, as during those days of hardship, we made friends easily and felt close towards each other.

The following five pages are extracts from the only edition of the *Vauvert School Magazine* which was printed in December 1940. Many thanks to Greta Carré (now Mrs. Ron Loaring) for the loan of it.

Greta Carré

The
Vauvert
CHRISTMAS School 1940
MAGAZINE.
- ❈ -- Nº1 - ❈ -

EDITORIAL

If a School, like a Church, consists of the persons
who are members, rather than of the building and its
furnishings, it will not be true to call this the Magazine
of Vauvert School.

We who now occupy these seats of learning are the
non-evacuated residue from a round dozen schools.
Not a few of us are scholastic orphans. Our one-time
class-rooms no longer re-echo with the healthy sounds of
jubilant youth, for there, sacks of flour and mute radios
hold their silent sway.
Others of us are in our own old rooms and find the unwonted
presence of strangers a little confusing.

But the strangeness of the first few weeks is now
wearing off. We are beginning to call our new acquaintances
'friends'. Our days have taken on the ordered sequence we
knew in the past and the wheels of study are turning once
more. We are beginning to look on Vauvert School, as it is
to-day, as 'Our School'.

We ask you, Reader, to look upon this effort
kindly. It is our first and we could hope it will be
our last. It will help to knit us more together into what
can truly be called a School and in days to come it may
prove a tangible link with our life to-day which may then
appear even stranger than it does now.

THE BLACK-OUT

It was quite dark but the unaccustomed black-out mad
it seem unnaturally so. Tall grotesque shapes were silhouet
against the sky . What could they be ?. Why,nothing but churc
steeples and tall buildings.
Pale blue lights,shimmering in the distance,told of labyrinth
of public ways,with perhaps a few belated people,from whom th
faint yellow moon would be hidden by intervening obstacles.

The night grew darker yet ; no more distant barking of
dogs and hardly any hum of traffic in the streets. The town
was only visible by its own faint light and not by the light
of heaven.

From my bedroom everything was so silent and still.
The moon was up but not a sound of living thing could be
heard upon the earth or in the air. Above me bent the blue;
dark,yet dewy and soft like the inverted bell of some
beautiful flower sprinkled with golden dust and breathing
fragrance.

Daphne Mahy .14 yrs.

BLUEBELLS

During the exciting season of Spring,usually on a
rough soil,shoot little green and yellowish stalks. On the
tops of the stalks shoot numbers of mauve bells which look
ever so dainty and fresh when the cool April showers fall on
them.
From afar off they look like a beautiful carpet of mauve and
blue.
After a while they droop and fade away and we do not see them
again until the next Spring.

Greta Carre . 9 yrs.

La chaume et la mousse
Verdissent les toits,
La colombe y glousse
L'hirondelle y boit.
Le bras d'une platane
Et un lierre epais
Couvrent la cabane
D'une ombre de paix.
L'onde qui s'éttend
Egale et sans fin
Fait entendre en cadence
Les ailes d'un moulin.

A LETTER TO FATHER CHRISTMAS

Vauvert School,

10th Dec 1940.

Dear Father Christmas,

It is perhaps too much to expect you to visit us this year. The sky over Guernsey is rather dangerous but if you could arrange to come in a Junkers 52 I suppose y would get here in safety. I hoping you will come: we have just had the chimney swept specially for you so that your white fur will not get dirty, and my pillow-case will be in its usual place at the foot of the bed so that you will be able to leave what you have brought without having to fumble much in the blackout.

Could you bring me some chocolate ?, I have not had any for three months. I would adore a good hunk of Dutch cheese also, and about two dozen eggs would be lovely, if you could get them across without breaking them. Even one egg would be very acceptable. Christmas dinner will not be its usual self without a leg of pork so if you could slip one into my pillow-case I would be very thankful.
I know all this is rather a lot to ask you but you usually manage to provide our requirements.
Oh,-and dont forget the fruit,-oranges, dates and nuts. Lemons are not so important.

I wouldn't mind a few toys but the townspeople are kindly taking on your job this year as regards toys and if you are only going to bring playthings, perhaps you had better not risk the trip. Anyway, I hope you have a safe journey, if you do decide to make the attempt, and that you will not find it necessary to camouflage your reindeer,

Yours,
Betty Boswell.

TIME MARCHES ON

THEN and NOW

G.F. Marriette

A SPY AT SCHOOL

Going back to the worry & concern of teachers throughout the 5 years, most concern was felt by mr Peter Girard (Headmaster of our school – Le Intermediate) during the early part of the Occupation. Writing his memoirs after the war (mainly connected with our education) he was approached & introduced to a German Civilian by the Guernsey Education Council as a School-Master anxious to improve his knowledge of English. He wished to be allowed to 'sit-in' at lessons given at the school. mr Girard felt this was reasonable enough until he was unofficially informed by a member of our local Guernsey Police Force that this man was thought to be a member of the 'Gestapo'. From then onwards everyone was very careful with any conversation when he was about.

After a time he sought permission of the Education Council wanting to give lessons to the more advanced pupils, who eventually enjoyed taking part in plays he organised. Even though he seemed a pleasant man, he was treated with caution & there was a time when mr Girard felt most uneasy watching boys thoroughly enjoying themselves pelting him with snow-balls!

It was some 10 years after the Liberation & Occupation had ended that mr Girard received a letter from the German admitting he was a member of the 'Feldgendarmarie' (German Police) at the time, but also assured mr Girard he had no reason whatsoever to report him (nor us!) whilst at the school.

1942 ??   1941

Chapter Three

GAMES TO PLAY

On the whole, the German Soldiers quite liked and, I am sure, felt a little sorry for the Guernsey children. Many soldiers were young but the older ones probably had children of their own back in Germany. Hence, some had sympathy towards us. Out of doors pleasure was very limited for the children who lived in the town. We had very little garden at 'Rose Villa' and we were not allowed on the beaches as most were heavily mined. I cannot remember ever playing on our park. I expect my mother had very little spare time to take us and I am sure she would not have allowed us to go there alone. We also were not allowed to play in our street where we lived as the 'Canichers' was always very busy with soldiers—plenty of activity so it meant Joyce (my sister) and I just had to find something different to get up to! It was probably nearly eighteen months after the enemy had invaded and when the family were hungry that we found a new game to play!

As soon as school was over we'd meet at home and take an old pram and go out together hunting and just looking for anything we could find, either to eat or anything that could be useful. We'd park our pram somewhere nearby, and with baskets more handy, off we'd go and usually end up with a basket full of potatoes between us, on a good day! This was our main thought—potatoes for the family. If boats were unloading we would wander every day after school to the stores either just down the road at the Truchot or we would walk through the town up to the 'Charroterie' Stores where the potatoes were being stored for the forces. These arrived in great quantities by boat, usually from France, and they filled these great stores to feed the thousands of troops. From the boats, they arrived by lorry or by horse and carts. Lucky for us the local 'boys' were employed. They had to shovel the potatoes into large wicker baskets and carry them on their backs into the

German soldiers parading past the Royal Hotel and along the Esplanade soon after they occupied Guernsey.

The familiar sight in the High Street to and from school.

large stores. Fortunately, the baskets got tilted and a couple of potatoes fell into the road or gutter each time! We were not slow in picking them up I can assure you! Looking back, we must have looked a strange bunch waiting to dive between horses hooves, carts and between lorries to collect one potato! Sometimes we would come home with maybe 5 or 6 each, another time perhaps a basket nearly full.

Joyce and I would usually stay for an hour after school but during our holidays we had more time to wait around. There were usually five or six 'locals' there, the times we were there waiting for the potatoes to fall. My sister and I, being the youngest and usually the only children, were usually lucky and probably got away with it the most! Hamel, the German in charge had to be watched though and we knew his mood as soon as he showed up! On a good afternoon he overlooked us standing there, other times he only had to shout once and we were gone! We would hide for a while at a house nearby (if at the Truchot) until he moved away, then back we came, never giving up—the catch was too precious. 'Hamel' was known by us and the local men who had to work under him for his shouting and red face as he did so. I am sure he was a boxer as a young man, as his nose was flattened, he was still a big man but then most of the Germans looked tall with rugged features to me then. He and the other Germans must have got fed up seeing us there I'm sure. The ordinary German soldiers on duty did not seem to mind us being there too much but Otto was the one person we dreaded to see there, though, gladly he was not too often in charge.

One particular afternoon I went too far by standing on the step board of a lorry as I thought no-one could see me. I was helping myself from the lorry and my basket was nearly full of potatoes when I heard a shout—my heart sank as I knew it was Otto, the very big Nazi who must have come out from the stores without me seeing him. The group of locals who used to be the 'regulars' had heard so many stories of him being brutal, we just tried always to avoid him. Well, on seeing me he started to run and chase me down Truchot Street shouting at the top of his voice, my, did I run! But with his long legs and massive big boots he eventually caught me up and gave me such a kick! My pride was really hurt and I ran home crying and rubbing my bottom! My father was furious and he wanted to go and find him. In anger, he threatened to find Otto on Liberation Day and he said he would kill him; all this time my mother was trying to pacify him and checking to see how hurt I was. Oh dear, why did I do it? I had never seen my father like it before, nor heard him say anything quite like this, he was always so placid. I think in that moment all his pent up feelings, the misery and boredom he felt and his uselessness of not being able to help the war effort caused his outburst. So many times, I remember, he would go upstairs during the light evenings and look out onto the harbour and islands and

Train at the bottom of Bosq Lane carrying cement to the north of the island.

wish so much he could help the war in some way; often he would tell me this. Now one of his daughters had been kicked, no matter if she deserved some punishment, it should not have come from this Otto. The look of him was enough for Dad to dislike him, and so many others felt the same about him. He was a familiar figure in his Nazi khaki uniform, walking to and fro through the Canichers, he always had a horrible smirk on his face—he looked what he was, a brute and, with being such a large, heavy man, with big shoulders and a big moustache, it made him stand out from all others. Although Dad would liked to have had a 'go' at him (Dad was also over 6ft. tall), he could not say a word and kept his tongue, but he never really forgave him. For myself, I was badly bruised, but this incident did not put Joyce and I off. I just made sure we kept to the gutters, always! And that was an order from Dad I meant to keep! Also, I should add, the black bottom was easier to bear seeing as I still had those precious potatoes!

Even having some potatoes Mum never wasted anything. One day we would eat the potatoes—the next day we ate the peelings. Mum must have been a genius to cook and to make do for nine in the family with next to nothing, it must have been a constant headache for her; so my sister and I just had to help in our small way. After my incident by the way with Otto, we also found that the story of him kicking an elderly man again at the stores was true, it happened to a Mr. Stevens, a nice quiet man, whom we knew also at the Potato Game. Before we thought maybe it was a 'story' made up, as there were so many rumours always going around the island, but no, not this time and this made Otto all the more unpopular.

At this time I can well remember the little pile of potatoes gradually getting bigger on the floor of our small attic room upstairs. Mum and Dad were able to help out many friends and relations, giving them a good feed. Joyce and I carried on collecting for as long as we could and while the going was good. It was probably for over a year to eighteen months or maybe a little longer.

Joyce and I both remember these days very well and it may seem strange to readers, but we enjoyed our 'game' and we enjoyed the end product more by knowing there were a few less for the Germans to enjoy!

COLLECTING AND COOKING

Cabbage was the main compliment vegetable and the only one Mum could get and even now I well remember the horrible taste of it! It was cooked all night in a large Bean Jar (a large earthenware casserole that local families have used for many years to cook their traditional Guernsey dish called 'Bean Jar'—hence the name), and cooked in a bakehouse down in the Pollet. With our pram, we would collect either one or two jars and, although we ate it, it tasted awful as it had been simmering for so long in the large ovens. This all helped the gas allowance which at times was little.

Joyce and I never seemed to go anywhere without our old pram, what would we have done without it! Also Mum of course, she borrowed it whilst we were at school! She never went anywhere without it, everyone knew 'Glad' and her old pram.

As soon as school was finished all our friends went straight home, my friends all lived in the country parishes so naturally their parents did not want them to have to walk or cycle unnecessarily, hence we never seemed to play after school like the children of all ages have always done and nowadays take for granted. There was never a Mum or Dad handy with a car to see children home safely, so most days after school we ended up somewhere different rather than always staying at home. I saw to my homework after tea, most times by candlelight, then usually bedtime was very early.

During our outings we actually made a little money by collecting acorns. There were none around our home so usually we used to walk to the Foulon Cemetery, collect quite a few, then sell them to shops. They were then roasted, ground and eventually sold as coffee. Carrots and parsnips were also grated and roasted and sold as Carrot Tea and Parsnip Coffee.

'Rose Villa', where we lived, was so central for everywhere. We made frequent visits to the Piette Saw Mills just a 5 minute walk away. We always seemed to manage to bring home a few pieces of wood from here, also sawdust shavings of wood and whatever else we could find.

Whilst at the 'Piette' one day a young German soldier came over to me and offered a large loaf! He could not speak any English and started jabbering in German. I must have looked surprised, not knowing what he was on about until I heard 'Bett' on the end of his jabber, with him pointing up the stairs! I was probably only 11 or 12 at the time and although I did not know much at this age, I quickly shook my head with a 'nein'!! I quickly hurried home with Joyce and I never mentioned a word to her or to anyone about this as if my mother or father had known about this offer, I definitely would not have been allowed to visit there again; wood or no wood it would have made no difference. As it was, I just kept clear afterwards of that particular store and was not nervous to go again. It was probably the feeling that the local men were always working there amongst the Germans and it was the same local men who helped and showed us where to find some shavings or sawdust; or, if lucky, a few pieces of wood. Maybe some of these men may read this account and will remember the two girls with the old pram and the shovel always ready. Should they do so, please be assured we were grateful at the time. Besides thanking these men, we must also give a special thank you to the men working at the 'Potato' stores. These men risked getting into a lot of trouble and maybe losing their jobs for giving us a wink and a tilt of the baskets when the Germans were looking the other way!

I don't think Joyce and I thought we would ever end up with cement in our pram, but we did, and my father was thrilled to have it, when we finally got home with it. This day we had just left the sawmills when we noticed a hundredweight of cement lying in the road near Salerie Corner. The bag had broken so there we were, in the middle of the road, shovelling up the contents which did not take us long to do. Lucky for us, there were no cars on the busy Esplanade, only horses and carts had to avoid us!

Another time we ended up in the 'Old Harbour', boats here occasionally used to unload coal, so one day, whilst the tide was out, we thought maybe there would be some lumps lying around and went to inspect. Yes, we were lucky, we handled the coal as quick as we could and filled the pram but my father did not recognise us at first when we passed him in the street, we were so black! He probably would liked to have disowned us at this time! All the time though Joyce and I were happy, there was nothing much else to keep us occupied.

Sea water was another commodity we collected. This again was handy to fetch as we were living so near to the waterfront. We collected this from the steps at Salerie Corner at high tide. Mum used it for cooking and she also simmered it in a large container sitting in one of the old large biscuit tins from before the war. The container with the salt water was surrounded with sawdust and lit—I remember the sawdust kept smouldering for many hours and this simmered the water to give us a very small quantity of cooking salt. Many local people used this method and it certainly worked! The sawdust and wood we managed to scrounge certainly helped as some alternative form of cooking had to be found as the allowance to householders was so small. Other older people though could not learn to help themselves. There was my mother's sister, and others like her, who quickly used up their gas ration for cooking and then were completely cut off until the next allowance. My aunt just could not accept the situation and this worry led her to have a serious breakdown with others to follow. My mother helped her and her family all she could but it was impossible to relieve the every day frustrations she just could not take.

My school days were Monday, Wednesday and Friday all day, Tuesday, Thursday and Saturday mornings only. Whilst 'butter milk' could be obtained, my mother and I used to walk every Tuesday and Thursday afternoons to the old States Dairy at St. Martins. It was an uphill climb all the way, but my mother and I used to take turns to push the 'old faithful'. We would have to queue for probably an hour or two for two large milk cans and, when home, Mum would simmer it again in the biscuit tin for hours and Mum found a recipe for a 'sweet'. Although 'butter milk' sounds like the best, it certainly was not, but probably there was still a little goodness to come out of it! After the simmering, like salt, it did end up very little but it all helped with our diet and although saccarins were rationed, they were indeed a blessing!

My mother and I would walk anywhere on the Island if there was the slightest chance of buying vegetables and very often walked as far as L'Ancresse. Families living on farms or in the country had more to eat than the town people. I am sure they could exchange, with others, their different root vegetables and of course they had land to grow these. We, living in St. Peter Port like most people, had a very small garden, with no room at all to grow any quantity of fruit or vegetables.

Whilst walking these many miles in the country it must have been a great effort for my mother to overcome her fear of horses. Everywhere were big, heavy horses drawing carts and she was absolutely terrified of them. The roads and lanes being so narrow there were many times when we had to jump over garden walls or run into houses when the horses looked a little frisky coming along the road. It was a shame for Mum, as really they were lovely horses, but she could never get used to seeing so many around. Many a time we would find two horses struggling to pull their wagons through the 'narrow' Canichers. This is purely a pedestrian walk (a short cut) leading from St. Julian's Avenue and at its widest is only 7 to 8ft. wide! These are the kind of stories we laugh about now and also at home later, but at the time were not at all funny!

Queuing at the French Halles, Market Street for vegetables. (Note the many bicycles and carts).

We were all certainly getting by even though maggots were included in our diet. Yes, there were plenty in our bread and many husks in our porridge. Each spoonful was nearly a mouthful of husks which we just could not swallow, only spit out! Carragean moss, collected from the beaches, could be bought and made into quite a presentable sweet and potato peelings too, we just could not waste anything. Grated Carrot Tea and Bramble Tea, also Acorn Coffee, were our drinks. Tom Jehan, the friend from school days, was one of many children who used to make some pocket money during school holidays by collecting bramble leaves and selling them to produce tea. I think Mums all over the island would have literally tried anything especially when it came to a better 'cuppa'.

Seeing there was just nothing interesting for children to buy from the shops, I was never given regular pocket money. The last small sweet ration was in 1941 and despite Joyce and I queuing for perhaps two hours, I can't remember if the shop, 'Collins', ran out of sweets before we managed to reach the counter! The one item that children did not seem to mind being so very scarce was 'soap'—but this was a real headache for the Mums as you can imagine.

One week I well remember Mum saying the whole ration for week was 2½d (old money of course) but despite the shortages people tended to keep going (although slowly) and I do not remember any epidemics breaking out amongst the local population. Maybe it was the main diet of vegetables which helped, although most times they were not plentiful and one had to queue hours at our market for maybe a swede or a parsnip. Queuing was an important part of my mother's life and, when possible, I would take over.

It was through my waiting at the stalls that led to a very welcome gift of vegetables given to me for many months. This very kind man who gave them was a Mr. Hubert who had a stall in the market and who lived in St. Andrews. He stopped me one day and asked if I would take my mother and go and speak to him. Apparently, I kept reminding him of his own daughter, Noella, who had evacuated to England in 1940 and who was very near my age. With tears in his eyes he asked if we would accept a few vegetables from him every weekend as a gift. What a lovely gesture and we were so grateful! Every Saturday, for many months, I used to go to market and talk to Mr. Hubert, he so wanted to know what I had been doing and how the family were. It must have been heartbreaking for parents to be parted from their children for five long years. If I had left Guernsey at 8 years of age I would have been a child, but five years later I would have returned a young woman. Parents lost all those precious years, not being able to see their children grow into adults and my mother and father understood very clearly why Mr. Hubert was interested and generous towards me. I wonder how parents felt being reunited with their children again after five years separation? Difficult

Joyce and I queuing for the last small sweet ration at 'Collins' Sweet Shop. The Pollet, 1941. (I am wearing white shoes and socks, with Joyce behind me).

to imagine, but what a relief and thankfulness. Some children, I am sure, must have changed in every way. As for Noella and myself, we have been mistaken several times for each other since and, through her parents, we have made friends.

Guernsey has always been known as 'The Friendly Isle' but it was even more so during the Occupation. We were all in the same boat so to speak and even though there were a few anonymous letters from the 'locals' to the Gestapo (German Police) regarding Islanders having maybe a little crystal set, a wireless, or joint of beef etc. etc. (more of this later), everyone tried to help each other and always tried to see the funny side of things. This is the one reason I wanted to dedicate my story to my mother, as during the whole time, despite everything, she remained cheerful, caring and helpful to everyone who knew her. I have really only appreciated her gift, and my father's too, since having two daughters and grandchildren of my own. I wonder how I would have coped under such circumstances?

Road signs at the bottom of St Julian's Avenue.

Chapter Four

GRANDPA'S PASTIMES

All this time there were still nine in the family at home; even though my mother's brother, Reg, had died. It was in 1941 when Uncle Reg had to have the operation to remove the bullet from his spine, but gangrene set in and he died soon after. Whilst he had a light job working down the harbour, he worked with a Mr. Mark Whelan who came to see my mother soon after my uncle's death and asked if he could come and lodge with us. He naturally found it difficult to cook and manage on such small rations as his wife and children had evacuated also and left him living alone. There was also a Cliff Holloway who lived alone in a house behind us and who Mum went in to see every day and usually managed to take him a meal. She especially kept an eye on him as he was so lonely and unhappy. His wife was away, like so many other wives, but to crown it all, Mr. Holloway received a Red Cross Letter during the early part of the Occupation stating their only son 'had been killed on active service'. With my mother's help he survived the Occupation but he never got over losing his son, Rex. His wife returned after Liberation but died soon afterwards. Mum again kept a watchful eye but unfortunately he committed suicide and it was mum who found him in the house. Perhaps you will realise now my mother was not the type to refuse another man in trouble even though Mr. Whelan was virtually only a friend of her late brother. Again the family was to be six males and three females right through the duration of the war.

I had remembered Mr. Whelan coming to the house soon after we had been occupied and bringing a large black collie, a lovely dog we called Billie. Whilst having to go to the island of Alderney soon after we were occupied, Mr. Whelan had to help clear up and Billie seemed to be the only 'local' left. All the local population had been evacuated so our Billie was welcomed and soon made a fuss of; the family all felt sorry he was alone. It was a sad day when he had to leave us as Mum and Dad said he needed so much to eat and there were just no scraps for him. We kept him for as long as we could but one day Mr. Whelan had to take him back. He eventually managed to place him on a boat going to Sark where, hopefully, he was looked after. Afterwards, we often wondered where or how he ended up.

We could not keep a cat either and the few that were found on the island were eaten by the Germans when eventually they were hungry and their provisions were cut off from France. This was very sad for children as it would have been a comfort to possess a pet and I know Joyce and I were upset when our Billie had to go; we knew and understood why but felt he had lost his owners and all the love and comfort he had been used to. It was just because the Germans had taken over everything! Why couldn't we be able to have a cat or a dog like we used to have before the Enemy came?

We kept bantams for a short while in our small garden but they only seemed to make a lot of noise, they did not get any bigger or fatter. We kept them until Grandpa killed them one day and feathered them. It was no problem for him to feather birds or to skin rabbits if need be because shooting birds and rabbits was the one hobby he was so keen on before the war started. He should not have surprised Mum one day when she came home from town to find him sitting and enjoying a plate full of sparrows! He was tucking into them in our back kitchen, hopefully he wanted to eat them up quickly before Mother returned home from town. He had caught these sparrows by a trap set up from a window and, with a sharp pull, somehow had choked the poor birds. This again was done only through Grandpa being hungry so really there was little Mum could say. She was probably grateful anyway that we could all have a little extra on our plates at lunch!

I can see my old grandfather now smoking his pipe, what was in it was anyone's guess! I only remember the smell was pretty awful! We used to have two or three rose bushes growing in the garden so he tried rose leaves dried and crushed. I think his favourite brand was his own though as we had a small conservatory in the front of the house which caught all the morning sun; Grandpa used to grow tobacco, hang and dry the leaves and he then just crushed them and hey presto! a puff, but if I remember rightly, he had to keep lighting up! He, like most men, would have tried anything to help out the small (if any) tobacco ration.

It was the same where food was concerned. Mum, like all other Mums, would have tried anything to fill up a corner. We children were always conscious of the fact also and never missed an opportunity when given the chance. One day I remember getting soup from 'Castle Carey' where Germans were living. We were passing and two Germans explained where we could get some soup. It did not take long for Joyce and I to run home and find the two biggest jugs we could find in the kitchen then run back as fast as we could while the offer was there. The one German had shown us the back entrance and then the long walk through the garden into the kitchen. This soup was a beautiful thick barley soup—I remember it well and we all enjoyed some for tea.

There was also one German who was occupying a house near the bottom of 'Bosq Lane' who frequently gave Joyce and I a slice of their 'dark' bread and jam whilst we were collecting potatoes. They definitely weren't all like Otto, I am glad to say.

Guernsey boats laid up at St. Peter Port harbour.

This was my father's identification card which everyone had to have.

Chapter Five

LAW AND ORDERS!

After the German Forces had landed, I remember the Island tried to resume its normal everyday life as best it could, but each day everyone wondered what was going to happen. On the front page of our 'Daily' newspaper were new Laws and Orders to be obeyed without question. I remember one of the first, 'by Order of the Commandant' was for all Fire Arms to be handed in, ammunition, guns and powder—to be handed in immediately. It was my old grandfather (what a character!), my mother's father, who caused the biggest scare during this time. Before the war his favourite hobby was shooting and he owned a gun and made his own cartridges and shells etc. Joe or Pop Collins, as he was affectionately called, was always to be found at 'The Rabbit Warren' whenever he had a chance. Well, the Germans soon put paid to this of course and he was most upset when seeing all firearms of every description had to be handed in at once. I remember well Grandpa 'blessing' the Germans for calling in his prize gun, the very last thing he wanted to hand over as he cherished it always. Well, Pop did hand in a gun and a small amount of gunpowder. Not knowing differently, Mum and Dad thought that was the whole amount of gunpowder and the only gun he had.

Mum and Dad probably did not think too much about these items, they were gone and that was that. Grandpa inwardly must have chuckled until one evening, about three years later, three German Gestapo burst into our house. They made it very clear they wanted to search the house and this they did from top to bottom in every room and also our small back yard. We all waited for the verdict but they found nothing and left the house muttering in German. After they had gone, Pop was outside checking inside a barrel of sawdust to see if his prize gun and powder had been disturbed. Grandpa had handed in a very old gun but kept his favourite well hidden amongst

My mother's identification card.

the rubbish! My poor mother nearly had a fit on the spot—no-one knew of it being there and if it had been found we would have been lucky in just being sent to Germany to a camp. The outcome would probably have been far worse! Grandpa really should have known better than to put all the family at such risk. 'We could have all been shot', I remember my father saying; but it was too late to let the Germans know about these items now, the punishment would have been the same and Mum and Dad dreaded the consequences. Mum and Dad and all the family had to keep quiet about it but my mother and father must have been really worried, thinking always if ever 'they' came again, would they find it?

'They' did come again, and again it must have been our lucky day. It was soon afterwards my grandmother, on Dad's side of the family, and other relations had been invited to join us for a little supper. My mother had recently left hospital after having an operation so it really was a get together and a little celebration.

(My mother helped me with this little story!) She said a friend, Charlie Smith, had somehow 'acquired' a cow from a farmer and he had walked through the night with this cow from the country to a coal yard near our home where it was killed by a local butcher and cut into joints for selling! These joints were hidden in an old chest of drawers and discreetly sold on the black market at a price you can just imagine! It was to be a treat for the family so Mum and Dad did not mind the expense for this time. We had just finished enjoying the meal, I can remember us all sitting around the table in our large room, when we heard the sound of boots coming up the path. Germans did not knock on either of our two entrance doors, not at these times. It was their custom just to burst in to living rooms and try to catch people unaware of their presence. Again, the Gestapo were to search from top to bottom and the yard, but again, muttered and spoke amongst themselves then walked out. What relief for my mother and father! Afterwards, I always remember, Mum and Dad thinking that perhaps someone had sent an anonymous letter about us having a black market joint of beef! No-one wanted to believe fellow Islanders would do such things, but unfortunately, it did happen. Hopefully, 'they' would not come again.

IN A TIGHT SPOT!

The only other time when Germans came to look over the house must have been during the early part of the Occupation. I remember it very well as I was at home alone with my mother. With this incident we were very fortunate to be allowed to stay in our home for the duration as it was only the very quick thinking of my mother that did it. The German Officers arrived at the door and wanted to look over the house. We knew why they wanted to look it over. Les Canichers, where we live, was a very busy street, there always being plenty of activity with German soldiers. It was also very important to live near the harbour, also the *Royal Hotel* and one house eventually later on, just opposite, was a departure centre or depot for many young soldiers being sent to Russia to fight. All these happenings were around us and Mum and I guessed that our home could well be in line for officers to live in. So, on this day when we spotted the officers coming up the path, Mum just knew what the outcome could be. With the road being so busy and with several of the larger houses taken over by Officers, it just had to be! They started with the top floor with us walking behind them and dreading with every step what the outcome would be, we knew with six bedrooms (sea views as well!) everything would be 'prima'. We knew this word well and they kept repeating it to each other. Coming down a flight of stairs and on to the first landing, my mother gave me a nudge and a wink and started groaning and moaning! She fell on to the floor and as I leaned over and muttered 'What's wrong, Mum?' she whispered 'Shh you fool – ooh, aah', the moaning seemed so real. The Germans looked concerned and asked 'Was ist laus? Was ist laus?' I answered and said Mum was sick, with that they must have believed it—they took a look at my face and my mother's and that must have been enough as off they went and we never saw them again. Quick thinking by my mother and what a blessing, as with all rooms 'prima' (lovely) our family would probably have had two or three hours to move out with just a few personal belongings. Clothes only—everything else the Germans would have stepped in and lived with for the duration of the Occupation. Many people experienced this and there was always the threat of it happening at any time.

There was always plenty of activity along our street. To us children it was comical to see the enemy all dressed up camouflaged in multicolours with large twigs and branches sticking out from their helmets. It was a usual sight to see them hopping over our garden walls and hiding behind our bushes.

At the headquarters opposite, the young German soldiers we used to see dreaded the thought of being sent to Russia especially if they had to go in the depths of winter with the weather so bitterly cold. Guernsey must have seemed like Paradise to them. Many a time we have seen these young soldiers hiding in our gardens amongst the bushes trying to evade the count when they were all lined up along the street. We did know of German soldiers trying to injure themselves to prevent going on active service and on to the Russian Front. They would deliberately fall over our garden walls into the road below and we did hear that two had died through their head injuries. We used to see the officers treating these men roughly and there was always plenty of commotion, but as regards to any receiving fatal injuries, nothing was written about such happenings.

The news was so important to the grown-ups during the war, but then grown-ups in Great Britain and everywhere felt the same, the difference living in our Island was we just could not feel free to listen to the 'news'. We had no wireless sets to listen to from 1942 but many people were hiding them in so many strange places and making little crystal sets, so news was still leaking through. My mother and father had two radio sets at the time the Germans called them in. One was a very old one which they handed in quite happily but they decided to hide and keep the better one out of sight. Why should the Germans have everything? they would say. As the days passed though, they decided it was too risky to keep it so had an offer from a friend, Bill Robilliard, (an undertaker) who would keep it in a coffin until duration! This he did with no-one the wiser. Later on, when the news was more encouraging, and when allowed, I often used to pop across to a house opposite to friends who lived there (a Mr. and Mrs. Stan De La Mothe) who had a little crystal set in their bedroom. I used to love fiddling with the 'whiskers' and listen to the news and sometimes, when I felt safe, listen to music. One day I looked out of the window to the garden below and there, watching me, was a German soldier! I quickly took the earphones off as he must have realised what I was up to. Gladly I never saw him again or heard anymore, I was just very careful the next time I popped over!

There were many times when Germans annoyed the local population. Maybe it was only for the families who lived beneath the 'Big Bertha's' at Les Cotils or The Blue Mountains (as we call them – see page 22). This is the steep road behind the Canichers which leads up to Cambridge Park and Beau Sejour. Although our curfew hours were 9pm or at times 10pm—some early mornings Germans would knock on our doors and tell us to get up and go out and leave the house, usually this order came at approximately 4am or 5am! Achtung! Achtung! would be the cry. All along the top of The Blue Mountains were several gun emplacements and very big guns (which we nick-named Big Berthas) and we would all have to leave the house while the practising of these great guns were carried out. 'Schnell' was a word they used so often—and that meant we had to move quick—at the double!

All doors and windows had to be left open and off we had to go. Very occasionally we were allowed to stay indoors as long as doors and windows remained open all the time. When having to leave the house we used to wander around and usually end up at an aunt's house up in Union Street, who incidentally had to have German officers billeted with her right through the Occupation.

Many instances like this occurred, I can well remember my father and uncles getting so frustrated about it all—they just couldn't help the war effort in any way and to be told where and when to go at such unearthly hours was a bit much to take at times. They were also so very bored too! On the whole though the German Forces respected the local population if they did what they were told. One incident I must add to their credit. Many Germans were living nearby at my aunt's house. She and her family had evacuated and one day an officer stopped my mother and, in broken English, told her he was being sent to Russia. He had apparently found many photographs in the house and recognised all of our family in some. He had seen us pass the house many times and wondered whether we would like to have them for safe keeping? He was concerned that other Germans might not look after them and be as careful when he left. We felt it was a nice gesture coming from a family man and was appreciated after the war was over.

A TREAT IN STORE

My father, Bill Finigan, was a very strong character, well liked and very respected by all who knew him. I have always been proud of him and even now I, and everyone, will always remember him as one of the best. He worked very hard as a young man and throughout the Occupation he carried on working, mainly carrying out small building repair jobs on properties. Everywhere he had to go was with a pair of trucks as his old lorry had to be handed over at the beginning of the Occupation. It was a case of making do but everyone understood and he was prepared to help anyone. One job he was asked to do did us a very big favour. He had a small job to see to on Herm and was given a special permit to go to the Island. He set off with the necessary tools and what materials he had scrounged or exchanged with other builders. Lucky for us, it was a very low tide and he took the opportunity of looking for ormers—the shellfish that local people love and now I'm afraid are rarely seen—well, Dad arrived home with dozens of these delicious fish hidden amongst his gear and my, did we and everyone else we knew enjoy them!

A different job for Dad now, but one that gave him a lot of satisfaction. During the early days after being occupied, one of his customers, a Mr. Branch, asked him to bury all his precious silver as he just knew the Germans would call for it all to be handed in. He lived in a very large, fine, old house in the Graveés and he knew the Forces would want to live in his home at some time. He was right, on both counts and unbeknown to the soldiers, they were continually walking over his treasures. Dad naturally kept quiet and was very pleased to recover it all at the end of the war in excellent condition.

Chapter Six

ENTERTAINERS AND CHARACTERS

At 'Woodcote', our home now in the Canichers, I have enjoyed taking many guests over the years, but only perhaps nine or ten at one time. During the Occupation the house was known as 'Rose Adele' and there were probably 40 to 50 prisoners of war (slave workers) called Todt living in this house, Russians, Algerians, Dutch, Poles and others. They were of so many different nationalities and all the local people felt so sorry for them. They lived in very poor conditions, with very little food and their clothing was very shabby and dirty. I shall always remember noticing their feet and the cord that was wound round and round to try and keep their broken shoes together. A lot of them merely had sacking tied around their feet. There wasn't much anyone could do to help them, but many a time, out of my father's small cigarette ration, he would take a chance that a German did not notice and pass one to them whilst in the street with Germans walking alongside them. They seemed to be under guard constantly and the Germans would have been very annoyed at seeing any kindness shown to these men. They always looked sad and miserable, not surprisingly, as living in conditions like they were, also having to work on Guernsey's fortifications would have got the best men down. I remember Dad and my uncles feeling sorry for them, like we all did, and we felt sorry that we couldn't even try and speak to them—it was all Verboten. Everything was Verboten, the grown-ups must have got really tired of it all.

One incident did get pass the German Verboten law and this concerned the Todt workers.

Every day these men used to queue at a 'soup kitchen' down at the bottom of Bosq Lane, near our home, where they were each handed a bowl of soup. We knew at least two local men who queued also and got their ration! One of these men was quite a character! He was Stan Workman, a very talented pianist, who I am sure will be remembered as a pianist at the local variety shows. My sister and I went to classes and learned how to tap dance and it wasn't very long before we were singing and dancing as 'The Finigan Sisters'. We enjoyed this very much and the variety shows were enjoyed by many people.

Stan Workman used to accompany us at some of the shows and he used to come to the house at lunch time from work to practice our routine, or just to have a tune on our piano. He could sit and just about play anything and everything without music. He was working nearby at the 'Truchot' where commodities were stored for the Forces. (Incidentally, next door was our Potato Store). Many a time he would arrive with a little something under his coat in return for perhaps a cup of tea and a bite to eat. One day in particular he gave my mother some soap powder which was in a small sack. She was, naturally, very grateful for anything, however small in quantity. As always, we saw him to the door and saw down our path a trail of soap powder! but it did not end at our gate, no, it carried on all the way back into the Stores! It did not take long to find the sweeping brush and get moving!

Stan did not seem to worry much and always seemed to be getting into trouble with the Germans. One never knew what his next move would be just to aggravate them. One evening, whilst playing at one of the local variety shows, he played 'There'll always be an England' then he decided to put the pedal down hard and play 'God Save the King'—one can imagine the expression of the German Forces who were always sitting on the front rows!

Many local men who were working for the Germans naturally would try and 'borrow' goods to maybe take home for their wives and/or children. If they were caught (like Stan was eventually) they were put on a list to wait their turn to serve their prison sentence as the Prison was always a full house and always over-crowded then. My cousin, Sid Collins, who was in his late teens at the time, stole a loaf from the Germans and was imprisoned for three months! The only time surely that it was felt an honour to serve a sentence! So Mr. Workman eventually got into prison after a long delayed wait, but I'm sure the Germans were not sure what on earth they had captured! Whilst not playing the piano, Mr. Workman, being shellshocked in the First World War, would make very strange noises and pull faces. Joyce and I thought this was strange at first, but when it was explained why he did it and could not help doing it, we understood. Strangely enough, when he concentrated on playing the piano, he controlled it. Well, whilst in prison, he continuously shouted to the guards and Germans, all day and all through the night he kept it up making these strange sounds and calling out. He was certainly playing up on his condition but being very clever too as everyone got absolutely fed

Joyce and I as the 'Finigan Sisters', appearing 1943 and early 1944.

up with him and he was soon transferred to a lock up room at the back of Palm Court Hotel, now known as Wyndham's Hotel. From our house we could see him standing at the window and could hear him shouting through the day and night. The Germans kept him locked up for two or three days longer but decided to release him. He was none the worse for his prison sentence, which was more than can be said for the Germans who came into contact with him! They must have been pleased and relieved to see the back of him!

Mr. Workman came back into the swing of things, but if I remember rightly, tried to behave himself after this episode.

Joyce and I were dancing together as an act during the shows of 1943 and up to June 1944. One show we were asked to dance in we chose red, white and blue material for our costumes, but that did not come off. I wonder why? It was amazing how attractive costumes were made to look with odds and ends of material which probably hadn't seen daylight for years. Also, a lot of parents who had children away were only too pleased to loan or sell their daughter's dancing clothes from when they had lessons before the war. In fact, all clothes were freely sold or exchanged through adverts in the local paper. With children being away, parents were only too pleased to help other children in need of clothing and shoes etc; especially so during the wintertime.

The Variety Shows we performed in were held mainly at *Candie Gardens* (then an Auditorium), the Lyric Theatre, the Central Halls and the old North Cinema. Sadly, not one of these buildings remain as entertainment places and The Little Theatre (the old Central Halls) unfortunately was burnt down only recently. The shows we danced in were either produced by Fred Leeder, Edward Le Huray, Billy Shepherd, Ernie Keyho, Bert Hewlett or Tony Chubb; also our dancing teacher who put on some very colourful and excellent 'Kiddy' shows, Miss Joyce Ferguson. These are the familiar names that come to mind but there could be others as there were many shows and I personally danced over 100 performances. Songs like "When the guards are on parade", "Tiptoe through the Tulips", "The Lambeth Way", "Ain't she sweet", "I can't give you anything but love", "My hat's on the side of my head", "The Girlfriend", "On the sunny side of the Street", "The Umbrella Man", and "You're the cream in my coffee" etc. Good old cheery, catchy tunes which I either sang and danced as a solo, a duet as "The Finigan Sisters', or with a friend, Brenda Le Lievre, or with maybe 5 or 7 other young people as a troupe. These Variety Shows and all entertainment put together for the locals were enjoyed very much and many excellent entertainers emerged. One in particular, as a comedian, was our dear Cyd Gardner. Everyone loved him, also Len Winterflood because they both made us laugh—this was just what the doctor ordered!

Joyce and I began our dancing during 1942 and whilst at the classes I made friends with a Peggy Bodkin. During September 1942 Peggy, together with her brother, mother and father (the latter being English born) were sent away very suddenly and eventually ended up in Germany. A little later on another friend, Margaret Gaudion, from the same 'Joyce Ferguson' Dancing School was deported with her family. Eventually, the two girls met up again in Biberach Camp and tap-danced together at the Prison Shows held there.

"Calling all Stars at the Regal Cinema", better known as the 'Odeon' since the war ended. Cyd Gardner presented a sell-out and gave the proceeds to the needy children of the island.

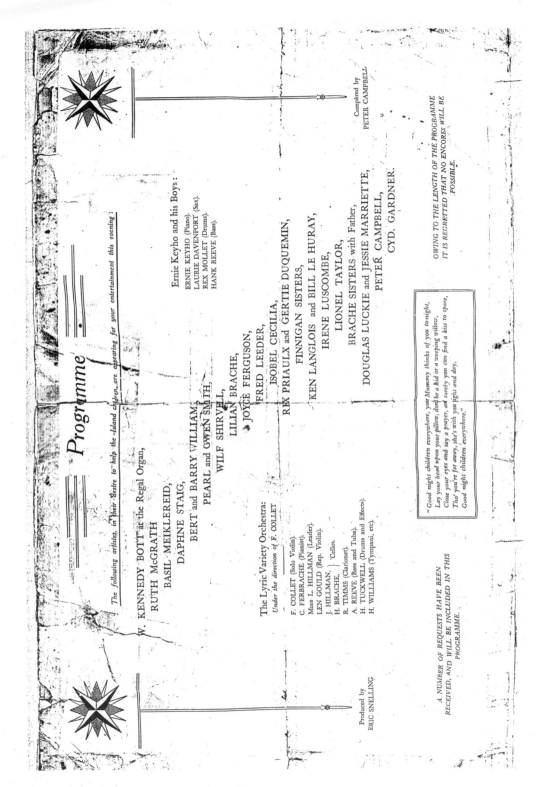

Programme

The following artistes, in their desire to help the Island children, are appearing for your entertainment this evening:

W. KENNEDY BOTT at the Regal Organ,

RUTH McGRATH

BASIL MEIKLEREID,

DAPHNE STAIG,

BERT and BARRY WILLIAMS

PEARL and GWEN SMITH,

WILF SHIRVELL,

LILIAN BRACHE,

JOYCE FERGUSON,

FRED LEEDER,

ISOBEL CECILIA,

REX PRIAULX and GERTIE DUQUEMIN,

FINNIGAN SISTERS,

KEN LANGLOIS and BILL LE HURAY,

IRENE LUSCOMBE,

LIONEL TAYLOR,

BRACHE SISTERS with Father,

DOUGLAS LUCKIE and JESSIE MARRIETTE,

PETER CAMPBELL,

CYD. GARDNER.

Ernie Keyho and his Boys :

ERNIE KEYHO (Piano).
LAURIE DAVENPORT (Sax).
REX MOLLET (Drums).
HANK REEVE (Bass).

The Lyric Variety Orchestra:
Under the direction of F. COLLET

F. COLLET (Solo Violin).
C. FERBRACHE (Pianist).
Miss L. HILLMAN (Leader).
LEN GOULD (Rep. Violin).
J. HILLMAN, } 'Cellos.
H. BRACHE, }
R. TIMMS (Clarionet).
A. REEVE (Bass and Tuba).
H. TUCKWELL (Drums and Effects).
H. WILLIAMS (Tympani, etc).

Compered by
PETER CAMPBELL

Produced by
ERIC SNELLING

OWING TO THE LENGTH OF THE PROGRAMME
IT IS REGRETTED THAT NO ENCORES WILL BE
POSSIBLE.

"Good night children everywhere, your Mummy thinks of you to-night,
Lay your head upon your pillow, don't be a kid or a weeping willow,
Close your eyes and say a prayer, and surely you can find a kiss to spare,
Tho' you're far away, she's with you light and day,
Good night children everywhere."

A NUMBER OF REQUESTS HAVE BEEN
RECEIVED, AND WILL BE INCLUDED IN THIS
PROGRAMME.

WE   THANK   YOU

In order to avoid intruding in the Programme may we here tender our grateful Thanks to all concerned in making possible the presentation of "Calling All Stars."

Cordially Yours,
Cyd. Gardner,
Eric Snelling,
Peter Campbell.

P.S.—In the r antime we'll be seeing you again in

"ANCHOR'S AWEIGH!"
— AT —
CANDIE GARDENS,
— ON —

TUESDAY,	THURSDAY,	FRIDAY,	SATURDAY,
July 13th.	July 15th,	July 16th.	July 17th.

THE LYRIC SPECIALITY SHOW WHICH HUNDREDS ARE WAITING TO SEE

STAR TYP., BORDAGE, GUERNSEY.

Mind you, my father gave a hearty laugh one evening and it cost him 10 Marks! It was at the Gaumont Cinema (now no longer a cinema) and the only time I went to see a film with my father, or with anyone else for that matter. Placed down the centre was a long dividing pole—one section of seats for the locals and the other side for the German Forces. Occasionally they showed a feature film with English sub-titles. Before this film they would show a newsreel emphasising how their Forces were winning the war. All of a sudden my father was amused at the propaganda and started to laugh aloud, directly the Germans who were guarding and on duty at the Exit doors rushed forward and demanded a 10 Mark fine on the spot! An expensive visit and we never went to the Gaumont again!

Apart from seeing the very excellent plays that were put on and coming to the Variety Shows, my mother's pleasure, when she could, was to play whist and 'Euchre' (a very popular Guernsey card game) at small drives that were held in the town and sometimes at Ozanne Hall. I often went with her for company and to watch, sometimes to play if needed to make up another table. One evening, whilst coming home through the town, usually before 9pm because of the early curfew, we saw a group of soldiers coming up the Pollet Street and looking rather merry and staggering a little. All were laughing and enjoying themselves when suddenly one came directly up to my mother and dug a revolver in her chest. We were so frightened and just stood frigid. We did not say a word but held our breath until he decided to drop the gun and place it back in his holster. He knew he had frightened us and that is just what he wanted to do; with that, they merrily went on their way and so did we, although quite shaken by the experience. We almost ran home after this and the small whist drives missed our company for quite a while. After this incident many older friends of my parents used to come home to play cards and if it was after curfew when they left, were pushed up over the garden walls to get home!

Gaumont Cinema, St. Julian's Avenue. Two minutes from our home. Featuring the film Victory in the West.

Troops listening with civilians to the German band in concert at Candie Gardens, 1940.

Chapter Seven

VEGA AND PARCELS

Time was passing slowly and food and other necessities were dwindling to near nothing by 1944. I can remember everyone thinking that we would soon be free when the British Forces landed in France and the news was the most important topic then, oh, but I do remember there were so many rumours. We were still surviving on meagre rations and I can well remember how very hungry we were. It had been quite a while since our 'Potato' game had come to a stop. The stores were almost empty now and no more boats were bringing potatoes or any other commodity for the troops, nor for us. Joyce and I had also stopped tap dancing, mainly because of the energy we were using and also because the Germans had stopped all entertainments of every kind by June 1944. The main topic of all the grown-ups was the events of the war and how the British Troops were progressing through France. Everyone was looking forward so much to being free, and it couldn't come fast enough. I can remember Mum and Dad saying we would soon be free and that soon we would have anything we liked to eat. Some sweets, chocolate, ice cream, fruit and food that really our age group could hardly remember, how they looked or, lesser still, how they tasted. We only knew Carraggean Moss from the beach was a kind of treat and cabbage and vegetables our main meal, as soup, even without meat or a bone, it could taste quite nice, but no variety at all. Bread was a funny colour with maggots most times but we had to eat what we could and probably could not remember the real taste of good bread and butter anyway. There was one consolation the local people had. If we were hungry, so were the German soldiers. We also had high hopes of the British winning the war and all the grown-up attitudes were much happier, also the most important thing, there were rumours of a Red Cross ship arriving with Food Parcels! We seemed to have to wait ages and still rumours but eventually at the end of December the S. S. *Vega* arrived bringing parcels of lovely food from New Zealand and Canada. Great excitement everywhere and the food tasted delicious. Our mothers must have been so thankful and I am sure many prayers were answered on December 27th 1944. The *Vega* was always a welcome sight after her first visit. We used to go to school very excited wanting to know what was in everyone else's parcels and what luxuries we were enjoying from them every day. We shall always be very grateful to the International Red Cross for sending us the *Vega* and for saving lives.

The Germans, during this time, were very hungry and a frequent sight in Les Canichers was to see them hunting through our dustbins trying to find scraps and bits and pieces from our parcels. All the empty tins were looked at and fingers rubbed inside to make sure nothing was left. I am sure many thefts occurred at this time as the Germans were indeed starving.

The Red Cross Supply Ship, Vega *steaming away back to Lisbon after her first visit delivering Red Cross parcels, bringing comfort and good cheer to every home.*

One Officer stopped me near our house and offered his binoculars, which he had around his neck, for a bar of chocolate. I called my father and he offered the German a taste of chocolate, about half the bar, and he handed over the binoculars very happily! They were the only German item we had as a souvenir and kept for a long time. Perhaps some might say Dad was wrong handing over some chocolate but at last he must have felt superior to the enemy. After nearly five years they had always had the upper hand, now they were beginning to realise the British were on top and we were going to win the war. At long last the time was right for Dad and I to walk away and smile.

Those Germans we used to see frequently passing along Les Canichers were getting thinner and thinner by the day it seemed, their uniforms were just hanging off them. Otto, the Nazi, was among these. I doubt very much if he could have run or kicked very hard at this time. Formally, he had been such a well and heavy built man with very big shoulders and features, now his body was bent over and very frail. As a whole too, the Germans were very despondent and low in spirits as the war was now swinging against them. When we were first occupied, and for a good while after, it seemed the Germans were always marching in groups and singing in the streets of the town. Now, all was quiet, no more shouting, no more singing their familiar song I.E.I.O. What it meant, I do not know!

I do know, and can remember, what going without bread for over three weeks meant though! Our last brown bread ration was February 12th 1945, but on March 8th we had a first ration of WHITE BREAD. I shall never forget collecting this loaf, to us it was just like cake, so big and white and tasted gorgeous. Below is a letter I wrote on March 5th 1945 to a dear friend, Mrs. Grace Mahy, who gave me this letter before she died. All through the Occupation her husband, Sid Mahy, worked at the harbour and managed very occasionally to bring a little treat home. They both had no children of their own and must have been fond of Joyce and I as they would share and make a special effort to give us a nice tea after school as often as they could.

These acts of kindness were typical of everyone during the Occupation as Mr. and Mrs. Mahy were strangers to us until they made themselves known when they first saw us dancing on the stage.

There was also another young person, a George Le Page, who made friends. He lived in the country at St. Andrews and would come all the way by his horse and cart to bring milk and a few vegetables whenever he could from his farm. To us 'townies' it was a treat to have a ride with George in his old horse and cart. I should add, mother kept well out of the way!

The family will never forget these kindnesses. We were so grateful at the time and Joyce and I so looked forward to the 'treats' and the invitations to Mr. and Mrs. Mahy's home at 'Tree-Tops'!

30 Camiolno
: St Peter Port.
Local.
5th March.

Dear Mrs Maby,

I am very sorry to hear you have been ill this last fortnight It was very funny but last night might in bed, I was thinking of you, and I made up my mind to write to you. When Joyce came home on Saturday within she said that you wasn't. then, I thought it was queer, but never thought of you being bad. Well, changing the subject, What do you think of the parcels? Aren't they lovely, ob soon ab they arrived, mummy opened the butter, chocolate and the porridge Joyce and I had this morning, and that delicious cocoa. We had 2 parcels with oatmeal and cocoa but none with 2-sugars. We are looking out for the "Vega," they say that was off Plaimont Points this afternoon. But you hear so many rumours, we don't know what to believe. On Friday we had 2 llb of Cod liver Oil and Malls falt of school children) which came by the Vega last time. Isn't it lovely.

Well, cheerio for now, cheer up ab the news in good, and we shall soon have bread. What is that? I shall come to see you to-morrow about 3 pm or just after.

With lots of love.
From Molly.
x x x x x
x x x x x x
x x x x x x x

Nothing this (this) book will be in
by this afternoon.

My letter to Mrs Maby which she gave back to me many years after and advised me to keep it as she had done.

This letter expresses a little of how I felt towards the parcels when I was 13 years old—cod liver oil and all!

Now that we were getting the Red Cross Parcels monthly and the British were getting closer, we were all so much happier, but I do remember the grown-ups getting impatient. Five years had been far too long and now it seemed they couldn't wait any longer to see our Forces land. That was all the talk, 'have you heard this?' or 'have you heard that?'. The news was so important—we had felt always so cut off with no letters, no magazines or newspapers and the crystal sets could not be listened to with ease at any time. It is very difficult now to imagine life without all these, should fog clamp down these days and no newspapers to read for a day, we are at a loss and soon feel we have missed out on something. Thinking back, it was the men who were so frustrated with it all. Dad had a little office on the top floor of our house and every light evening he would go upstairs for an hour or so and would sit glued to the window looking out to the harbour and just willing planes to come over and bomb. Just to relieve the boredom. During the latter part of the War, towards France, we could often see the sky lit up at night with flashes of gun fire and could hear the distant rumbling of bombardment, sometimes quite strong. Many a time the sirens would sound and the Germans could be seen to run and scatter for shelter, but no bombing, the risk being too great for the local population. There was one occasion when a mine was dropped in a garden accidentally, not 100 yards from our home. Luckily for us it did not go off but only produced a very large crater and no-one was hurt. Guernsey people were very lucky with regards to air raids. We often spoke and did worry and feel very anxious for the mainland population, also for family and friends away. It was terrible to see many planes in formation flying high over the island. Somewhere there would be many lives lost and much tragedy.

I can remember how happy everyone was one day just after D-Day when planes came over and bombed the harbour. Their objective was a submarine lying in the Old Harbour (which is now the new 'Town Marina') but unfortunately the Germans had decided to move it. There was a great explosion and most of the shop windows in the town were shattered. The children were very happy as a result as the school was closed for a few weeks!! This bombing highlighted the need to be remembered by the British, plus the excitement in those few moments.

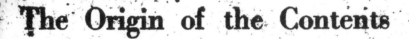

The Origin of the Contents

— OF OUR —

CANADIAN RED CROSS PARCELS

*And including a survey of the history and work
of the Red Cross Organizations, and
of the Order of St. John.*

❖ Emblems appear with ❖
permission of the Chairman
and Committee of the British
— Red Cross and Order of —
❖❖❖❖ St. John. ❖❖❖❖

Published by the

STATES INTERMEDIATE SCHOOL

QUI VEULT PEULT.

Net Proceeds in Aid of Red Cross Funds.

THE GEOGRAPHY OF OUR RED CROSS PARCELS

(I) THE CANADIAN PARCELS

CONTENTS

The Dominion of Canada.
Canadian Red Cross Flour and Biscuits from the Canadian Prairies.
Canadian Dairy Produce, including Dried Milk, Condensed Milk, Butter and Cheese from Eastern Canada.
Canadian Pork Products.
Fruit Farming in Canada, including the Production of Dehydrated or Dried Apples and Fruit for Jam.
The Dried Fruits of California.
New Brunswick Sardines.
British Columbian Salmon.
Canadian Red Cross Salt.
The Production of Citrus Fruits in the United States of America.
Red Cross Coffee.
Red Cross Tea.
Red Cross Sugar.
The Corned Beef from the Pampa. Red Cross Cocoa and Chocolate.
Red Cross Soap.

Compiled by Lower VI, Intermediate School, 1945

Editor — P. J. GIRARD, B.Sc. (Hortic.).
Sub Editor — JACQUELINE BREHAUT.

After the Liberation, appreciation was shown in receiving the Red Cross Parcels by producing an interesting 48 page booklet published by the States Intermediate School. Proceeds from the sale were in aid of Red Cross Funds and St. John organisations.

The project undertaken was to recall the origin and organisation of both these Societies and to study contents of the Food Parcels and to find out everything possible about them and about the places from which they originated.

The Canadian parcels were studied by a senior class of the States Intermediate School and this represented a term's work during the latter part of the Occupation. Many thanks to Jacqueline Brehaut (now Mrs. D. Stuckey) for the loan of the booklet.

LETTERS OF THANKS

SENT TO THE PRESIDENT OF THE INTERNATIONAL RED CROSS DURING THE PERIOD OF GERMAN OCCUPATION ON BEHALF OF THE CHILDREN OF THE INTERMEDIATE SCHOOL.

States Intermediate School,
Burnt Lane,
St. Peter Port, Guernsey, C.I,
March 3rd, 1945.

TO THE PRESIDENT OF THE INTERNATIONAL RED CROSS.

Dear Sir,

I must begin by thanking you for all you have done for our islands. One has to be in a position such as we are, to be able to appreciate fully the true food value of the Red Cross Parcels.

The Cod Liver Oil is also very good for us, because many of the children are losing weight; and besides it is a treat to eat it.

For three weeks we have been without bread, and so we welcome the Parcels even more than before, especially the Canadian ones, because they contain biscuits, which we can have for breakfast. Another advantage, which some of the Canadian Parcels have, is the soap. We have had no rations of that for several months.

But now people look more cheerful, because the relief ship, the *Vega*, is expected in two or three days' time, laden with flour for us. Probably it will be welcomed with shouts and cheers by the people anxiously watching for it. This happened the first time it came to Guernsey.

The reason why people await it so anxiously is because there are hardly any potatoes or vegetables left in the Island.

Today, as I went to the grocer's shop to fetch my fourth Parcel, I met many people, wearing smiles on their faces and wheeling small carts carrying their Parcels home.

The children especially were eager to get home because opening a Parcel is as exciting as opening a Christmas stocking. The first thing which they look for is the chocolate. For nearly five years, except for an occasional ration bought by the States from France, we have had no sweetmeats of any kind.

Since Christmas-time we have been without gas, and it is very difficult to find the necessary fuel with which to cook. Also, for one week we have been without electricity.

But I can assure you that every person in Guernsey feels grateful for all the Red Cross Society and the Order of St. John have done, and we will never forget it.

Again thanking you,
Yours faithfully,
ENID LE TISSIER.

SENT TO THE CAPTAIN OF THE *VEGA* AFTER OUR LIBERATION

States Intermediate School,
Guernsey, June 4th, 1945.

Dear Sir,

On behalf of the Intermediate School, we should like to thank you and your crew for the services which you so bravely rendered to our Islands during the latter part of the war.

We cannot fully realise the dangers and difficulties which you must have had to face for our sakes. All through the years to come you may feel quite rightly, that you have been instrumental in saving the lives of thousands of people and it is with extreme gratitude that we think of the work of the good ship *Vega*.

Probably, never before has one ship meant so much to so many people. We cannot hope to make you understand how eagerly we tried to follow the fortunes of your ship through the scanty information we received. Given the opportunity we could amuse you by recounting the wild rumours of disaster that were spread abroad concerning your ship, but every time the good ship *Vega* sailed into our harbour, bringing succour and sustenance. We trusted you and our trust was never belied.

In sending this letter of thanks, we feel that we are voicing the thanks of enormous numbers of Channel Islanders who will never forget how the *Vega* saved them from death.

We remain,
Yours sincerely,
BETTY GILROY,
ENID LE TISSIER.

A German drawing of St. Peter Port Harbour. A boom is stretchered across the pierheads and German vessels are shown at the quays. (Reproduced by permission of the Royal Court of Guernsey).

Chapter Eight

LIBERATION

Now every day was one less to tolerate under the German rule. Rumours were still going round as they had been all through the years, but after waiting and praying for so long, our 'day' was soon to come. The heading on the front page of the 'Guernsey Press' told us we could 'fly our Flags' at 3pm May 8th. At last, what excitement and relief to Mum, Dad and everyone. Upstairs, Mum told us to get the flags out, ready to fly them across the street. With a radio getting an airing at long last, neighbours and the family got together in the street to listen to our dear Winston Churchill giving his famous speech. We did not worry if Germans were around us or whether they were passing by, the radio was in an upstairs bedroom window and we were gathered together in the road. I remember him loud and clear, "Our dear Channel Islands will be free".

This was the afternoon when I took the "Liberation" Photograph with an old Box camera Mum and Dad had not handed in and can only assume there was a film inside all those years before.

May 9th was to be our day. I don't think anyone could really sleep well that previous night, we all had so much to look forward to. I remember Joyce and I wakening early around 6am, our first thought was to look out the window. We soon woke the household as clearly we could see the ships in the distance. My mother, sister and myself soon got dressed and dashed off down towards the harbour. At the Weighbridge Islanders were gathering, but seeing as we were down early, we were just behind the gates and the constables who were to keep us off the harbour. The harbour being out of bounds and heavily mined! Our eyes were glued to the road as we could not see if the boats had come into the harbour. We all wanted that first glimpse of British soldiers. By this time an hour seemed ages, but we

The Royal Navy anchored just outside the Harbour after Liberation Day.

all waited patiently until that small party coming up the harbour got bigger
and closer and we just could not hold back our excitement any longer. They
looked wonderfully smart with bayonets held high—we all ran as fast as we
could and I was among the first persons to greet them. We were hugging
them, kissing them, laughing and crying at the same time. Even the soldiers
were overcome too and I am sure they had never seen or felt anything like
it before. Everyone was overwhelmed with relief. The soldiers had their hats
and bayonets flying in all directions, it was a wonderful moment and if I live
to be 100 I shall never forget it. All day, 9th May 1945, was a wonderful
day! My sister, mother and myself never saw each other again that day until
about 8pm when we decided to go home. Although our home was only five
minutes walk away from the town, it never occurred to me to go home at all
during the day. My father was also lost in the crowd and in the excitement.
All Guernsey must have been out and there were tears, singing and laughter
everywhere. It is difficult for me to put into words the happiness I felt, as
young as I was, I felt such deep gratitude. I never dreamt I could feel such
happiness and exhilaration.

My mother (centre front), Grandpa (far left) and my father (standing at the back) together with friends and neighbours in jubilant spirits after hearing Mr Winston Churchill on the radio, May 8th 1945, Les Canichers.

Excited Islanders at the Weighbridge. Morning – Liberation Day, 1945.

EARLY NEXT MORNING, MAY 9TH!

Islanders gathered at the Weighbridge greeting the first 22 artillery men. I am amongst the few (facing centre) at the Harbour. Although disarranged after we ran to them, bayonets can clearly be seen. (Shot taken from the film – hence the photograph not clear but thanks to William (Bill) Bell and the Guernsey archives for permission to print).

Saying 'Farewell' at the Harbour to our Liberation Soldier friends.
Back row (left to right): Mrs Edie Masterton, Taffy Owen, Taffy Collins.
Centre row: Myself, Mum, Joyce, my aunt and uncle (Mr and Mrs Sid Collins) and Berni.
Front row: Taffy Ralph, a friend, Mrs Battrick (up from Jersey) and cousin Betty.

All through the 5 years, the people on the Island had felt very close having to cope with hunger, boredom and frustration, they shared everyone's troubles and tried to help each other, now it was time to rejoice and be happy. All the Forces that landed were wonderful too, sharing in 'our day'; we had no cares that day, just thankfulness and love for our British whom at last had come.

Many radio reporters were in the town interviewing people but most of all I remember the hearty singing. I seemed to want to be in several places at the same time, there was so much excitement going on, but it was the case of following the crowds most of the time as all the streets were packed in the town. I remember very well I ate only a couple of biscuits all through the day and these were given to me by a soldier; a sailor also gave me an orange! I just flung my arms around him when I thanked him, I was so thrilled. Mind you, I hadn't a clue to what it tasted like or how I was going to tackle it!

We were all very excited when we eventually arrived home and just did not want 9th May to end, but of course we had everything good to look forward to. My mother, incidentally, had cheered and sang so much she lost her voice completely for a few days and for months and months had a strained and croaky voice! She always said it was all worthwhile as in all her 80 years she has never known a day like it before or since!

I am pleased to say not one of our family saw another German soldier on this day or afterwards, not even Otto. Maybe just as well, but my father had long forgotten his words in the 'heated moment' and now for Guernsey, and for him, everything was looking 'prima'.

On reflection, and remembering my dear mother and dear father's words, we were very grateful to have come through quite well and, having remained together, we were still a very close family. Despite all the worry, hard work and tension, not once during the five years had I seen my mother down. Worried and frightened, yes, but she was always cheerful, never any different. She really did not have much time to be miserable with nine in the family to keep happy and to feed, she just had to keep going. My mother's job was to queue and to cook, my father's evening job every night was cutting vegetables into cubes for the next day's soup. My father's help and love was my mother's comfort I am sure, and his support was always within reach. They had a wonderful happy marriage together.

Another consolation Mum and Dad had and were grateful for, and thankful my sister and I had not been evacuated, was at least Mum and Dad did know where we were, how we were and what we were doing. We helped the food ration and the heating in our small way and also helped by bringing home our young friends. Many a time I would play the piano with Mum and have a sing-song. There was no order against this and it all helped the time pass by. Mum and Dad were grateful too that at the end we were

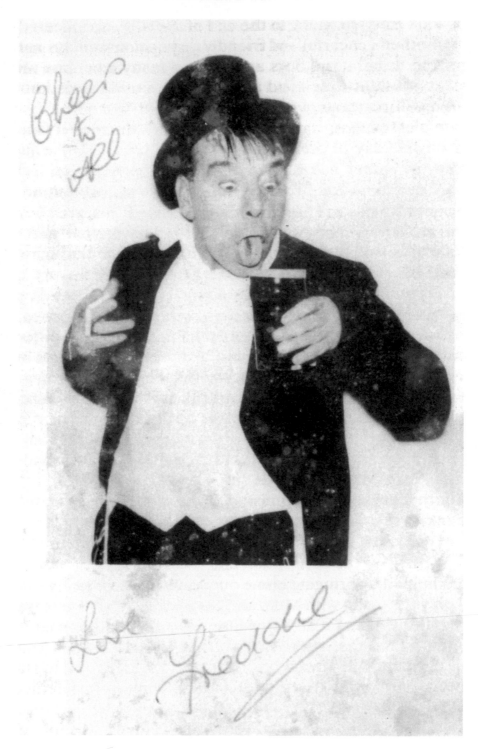

Freddie Frinton.

all together and grateful that all the family had been born and had been allowed to stay in Guernsey. We often thought of friends who were interned to German Prison Camps. There were many people who were made to leave the island and amongst them English-born friends of my mother's and father's. After they left very suddenly, we had no more news of them and I remember very well Mum and Dad being very concerned. I often thought of my old friends too as going to Germany seemed like going to the end of the world to me then.

My mother's cheerful and friendly disposition soon brought in many of the 'Liberation' boys and we had many a happy evening with plenty of tales to tell and a sing-song around the piano. The majority of these boys were Welsh and had wonderful voices. Amongst the friends was Freddie Frinton who came over to entertain the troops in 'Stars in Battledress' and will be remembered later as a comedian on the television in a series with Thora Hird. It was whilst Joyce and I were playing ball in the Canichers that he joined in and was welcomed in homes like many others. I remember well us walking with him to show off 'Les Vauxbelets Chapel' and drinking milk (him also) straight from the cow when offered some by a farmer. I think we all looked upon these men as 'Super Men' and we admired them all. We kept in touch with Freddie until he died and still write to two others who are living in South Wales. One of these 'Liberation boys' is now 76 and is a retired miner. He, together with his wife, spent a holiday in Guernsey last September. They have frequently come back with very happy memories of the Island and all the friends they made.

Chapter Nine

LETTER OF PRIDE

After the celebration of Liberation Day had died down a little, my father suggested I should write to the man we felt we owed so much to, Winston Churchill. Every Islander felt so thankful he had given us our freedom and we were full of gratitude towards him. I sat down and wrote, little expecting a reply, but was so thrilled when an envelope arrived with the '10 Downing Street', Whitehall and PRIME MINISTER stamped on it. I was so proud and you can see the write up printed in the 'Press' the next day on page 87.

To this day, I have treasured this letter from the man 'Our Hero' at the time to whom the Islanders owed so much and to whom we all felt and still feel great affection for now. It was disappointing for us that he was unable to visit the Islands after we were liberated, but we were all thrilled to see our King George VI and Queen Elizabeth when they both paid a visit during June. We, the schoolchildren, had pride of place in seeing them both. There was really great rejoicing and excitement for weeks after the war ended when all the families were re-united gradually together again. Also there was great excitement in our home because my sister was one of 20 schoolchildren chosen to spend a holiday in London and to represent the Guernsey Schools in the Victory Parade. All of us schoolchildren had been given a 'Liberation Day Medal', a gift from the Guernsey States to commemorate our Freedom. Each child who went away were very proud to wear their medal at the Victory Parade and, together with their teachers, were given a wonderful holiday in London.

My childhood days were certainly different and all these experiences I remember very well. Strangely enough, I do not remember any of my birthdays during these five years, neither do I remember any Christmases. The family made up for these times after and we had wonderful times when the aunts, cousins and friends returned to the island.

10, Downing Street,
Whitehall.

I have been deeply
touched by all the messages
of good will which have
reached me at this time.
Thank you so much for your
kind thought.

Winston S. Churchill

May, 1945.

My letter from Winston Churchill.

MAY. 26th 1945.

PRIME MINISTER

Sends Message to Guernsey School Girl

Thirteen-year-old Molly Finigan, of 30, Canichers, St. Peter-Port, was the proudest girl in Guernsey yesterday: she received a reply personally signed by Prime Minister Winston Churchill to her message of gratitude at our liberation.

On May 9th Molly sent the following post card Souvenir of Liberation and Re-union to the Right Honourable Winston Churchill: " On behalf of all schoolchildren, including myself, we express our gratitude and thanks for our liberation and freedom after five years of hardship. May God bless you and your loved ones. I remain a faithful admirer.—Molly Finigan (13 years) ."

Little did Molly expect a reply. But yesterday back came a message from the Prime Minister, bearing his personal autograph. It read: " I have been deeply touched by all the messages of goodwill which have reached me at this time. Thank you so much for your kind thoughts."

WINSTON S. CHURCHILL.

Write up in the Guernsey Evening Press, *May 25th 1945.*

I have never forgotten the happy school days at Vauvert and at the Occupation Intermediate School. I shall never forget the many happy hours and fun we had with Joyce Ferguson and with friends at Tap Dancing Classes.

Ebenezer Church holds pleasant memories too. The Germans did not stop Islanders attending church. Everyone was friendly and in the same boat, so to speak, and all made the most out of life.

Although I was young throughout, at no time did I feel nervous or frightened to leave the house. I used to take charge of my sister and our pram and off we'd go. I think that if we had been stopped going on our little jaunts, Joyce and I would have been upset. Obviously we were very proud with our efforts to lessen the German ration and naturally had to keep our game a big secret! I am sure it was only our young and innocent looks that helped us get away with everything! It must have been the Mums and Dads of Guernsey who were the most worried and anxious at this difficult time for the safety and the well being of their families. Many Dads also were very worried as they were separated from their wives and children, those from whom they seldom heard as the Red Cross messages were very few and far between, they just lived to be re-united once again.

To sum up our Liberation Day and feelings, these last words must come from my mother who sent this message dated 11th May 1945 to dear friends Edie and Billy Willcox living at the time in Yorkshire. Luckily and thankfully they had decided to evacuate back to England in 1940 (as they were English born) and we had received little news from them during the 5 years of the Occupation.

Our dear Aunty Edie had saved this very first message from the family until she died nearly forty years later.

It was many years ago (before the war started) Mr. and Mrs. Wilcox arrived to live in Guernsey from Yorkshire and on their very first day my mother and father made friends. Their very good friendship lasted all through their lives and as far back as I remember, even as Joyce and I were toddlers, they became a much loved aunt and uncle. During the war, Aunty Edie worked very hard and was an ambulance driver all through the Blitz and Uncle Billy was in the Army. After returning to the Island, many Islanders will remember they built and ran 'Peary Nook Tearooms' at Vazon for many years. Through helping her during these years and with encouragement and help from my father, my husband and I have successfully run a Guest House for 23 years. My sister, Joyce, has also had a Guest House in Cordier Hill for many years, is married to Mr. Walt Baudains, and they also have two children, both married.

Over the years, we have met so many people who have wanted to know of our Occupation that I just had to tell our story. I do hope you have found the reading interesting and have enjoyed hearing of the family 'goings on'.

Canchers

Souvenir of Liberation and Re-Union,
Guernsey, C.I.

Correspondence to be Written here

my Dear Edie
+ Bill. Thank God
we can write to
you and the
British are here
We are all well
hope you are,
longing to see
you all. It is
like Heaven to
be free. I have plenty
to tell you Best love
x from x Glad, Bill x molly &
&o &E

First letter to Aunty Edie after the liberation.

Never forgetting the lives that were given and the suffering still endured for our freedom, mother joined the British Legion in 1947 and each year after the war she raised money selling poppies for Remembrance Day. For many years at the Arcade Steps, playing an old Barrel Organ, and in Boots doorway. Not for an hour or two but all day from before 8.30 am in all weathers. Being so very popular and well liked by everyone she raised a considerable sum of money over the years.

This photograph was taken in November 1984 when mum was 84 years of age.

Printed courtesy of the *Guernsey Evening Press.*

My mother was cheerful into her 80s, I might add, despite being a widow for 13 years. She lived with my husband and I at 'Woodcote', Les Canichers, St. Peter Port for several years. We have two daughters, Carol is the younger and a Registered Nurse living at the moment on a boat (what freedom!) on the South Coast of England. Our married daughter, Sally, is now Mrs. Michael Howlett and they have two children; a son, Ryan, and a baby daughter, Carly. Together they live nearby at 'Rose Villa' on the opposite side of the street at the home which, for me, will always hold wonderful childhood memories shared with the best of parents.

Now, forty years on since our Liberation, may our children, grandchildren and future great grandchildren be blessed always with continued Peace and Freedom.

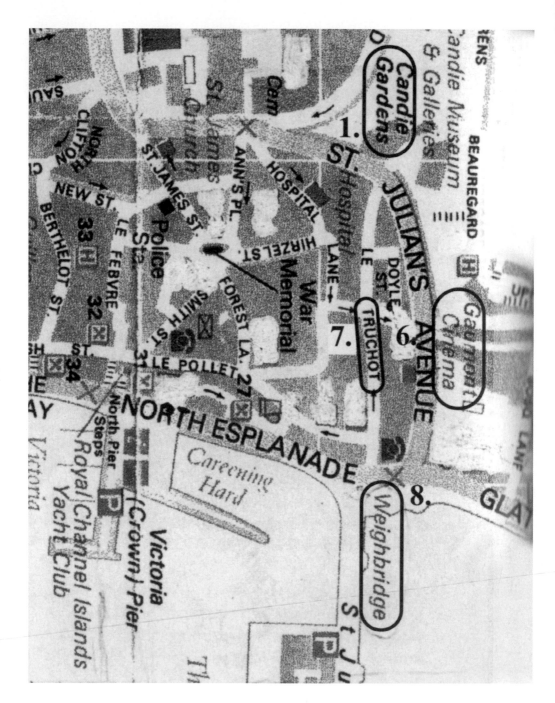

1. Candie Gardens and Museum
2. Les Cotils (Blue Mountains)

3. Les Canichers (Rose-Villa and Woodcote)
4. The Piette Saw Mills

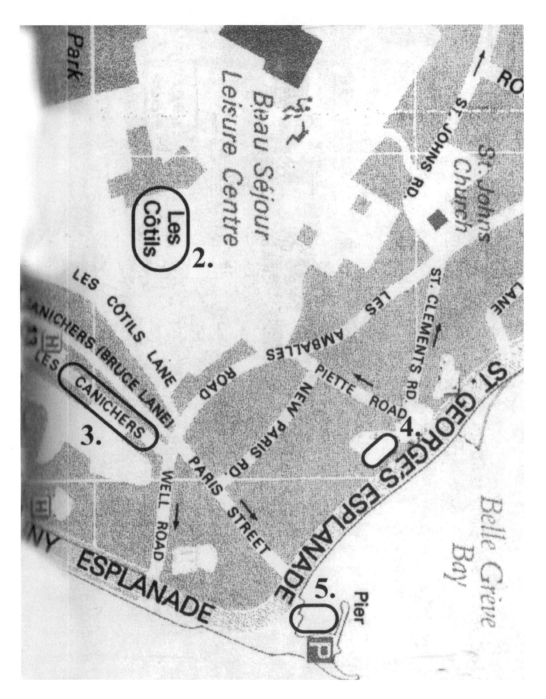

5. *La Salerie Harbour*
6. *Gaumont Cinema (now offices)*

7. *Le Truchot*
8. *Royal Hotel (now offices) (page 34)*
   The Weighbridge (pages 78-79)

8th June, 1946

To-DAY, AS WE CELEBRATE VICTORY, I send this personal message to you and all other boys and girls at school. For you have shared in the hardships and dangers of a total war and you have shared no less in the triumph of the Allied Nations.

I know you will always feel proud to belong to a country which was capable of such supreme effort; proud, too, of parents and elder brothers and sisters who by their courage, endurance and enterprise brought victory. May these qualities be yours as you grow up and join in the common effort to establish among the nations of the world unity and peace.

George R.I.

Further Reading

The following sequels are available:

Reflections of Guernsey

and

A Time for Memories

Knowing readers wanted more stories I have continued with events of the German Occupation of Guernsey in my second book and also with letters of interest from Germany. I first published *Reflections of Guernsey* in 1993 after my dear mother died in 1991, finishing her story and mine with an up to date account of our family in 2007.

My third book, *A Time for Memories*, was first published in 2005. I wanted other accounts of the Occupation by older friends I knew who had a story to tell. I was also priviliged to print the Dame of Sark's (Mrs Sibyl Hathaway) memoirs in her own words, with photographs. The Channel Islands' news to the U.K. were welcomed and printed soon after and during the Occcupation. Censorship was severe, but some Red Cross coded messages that were sent got through. Remembering deportation and Interment Camps and our gratitude for the ship *Vega* saving lives and bringing food to the Islands eventually.

Liberation Day, 9 May 1945, remembered and in 1995 retold by veterans of Task Force 135 – our heroes at the time – who came to the Island to celebrate with us 50 years of freedom.

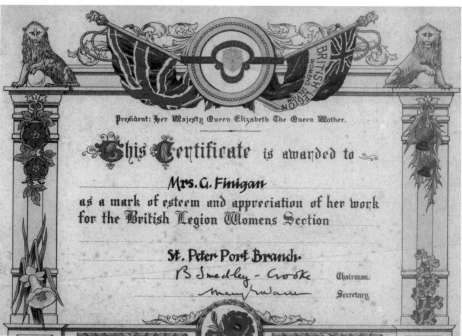

Both certificates were presented to my mother, together with a poppy 'brooch' which I wear with pride when collecting money, continuing in some small way her wonderful efforts to both the Poppy Appeal funds and the British Legion.